Wow, That's Woolly!

ANGORA RABBITS

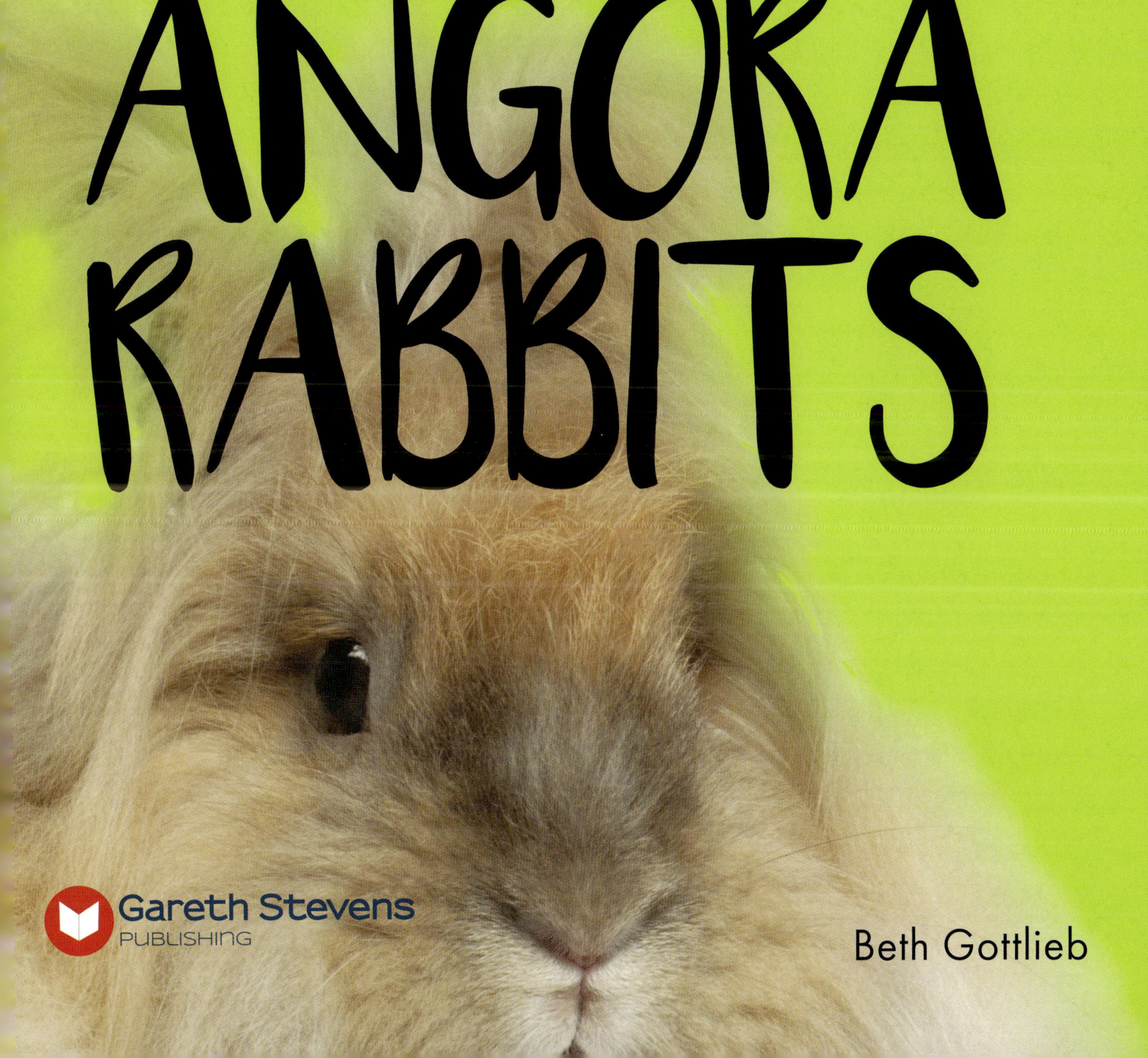

Gareth Stevens
PUBLISHING

Beth Gottlieb

Please visit our website, www.garethstevens.com. For a free color catalog of all our
1-800-542-2595 or fax 1-877-542-2596.

Library of Congress Cataloging-in-Publication Data
Names: Gottlieb, Beth, author.
Title: Angora rabbits / Beth Gottlieb.
Description: New York : Gareth Stevens Publishing, [2023] | Series: Wow, that's woolly! | Includes index.
Identifiers: LCCN 2021055355 (print) | LCCN 2021055356 (ebook) | ISBN 9781538279366 (set) | ISBN 9781538279373 (library binding) | ISBN 9781538279359 (paperback) | ISBN 9781538279380 (ebook)
Subjects: LCSH: Angora rabbits--Juvenile literature. | Wool--Juvenile literature.
Classification: LCC SF455.A5 G68 2023 (print) | LCC SF455.A5 (ebook) | DDC 636.932/2--dc23/eng/20211201
LC record available at https://lccn.loc.gov/2021055355
LC ebook record available at https://lccn.loc.gov/2021055356

Published in 2023 by
Gareth Stevens Publishing
29 E. 21st Street
New York, NY 10010

Designer: Olivia Lo Sardo
Editor: Kristen Nelson

Portions of this work were originally authored by Marigold Brooks and published as *Angora Rabbits*. All new material this edition authored by Beth Gottlieb.

Photo credits: Cover Murbansky/Shutterstock.com; book art (rabbit silhouette) Kolesnikov Vladimir/Shutterstock.com; pp. 4, 8–9, 12 cynoclub/Shutterstock.com; p. 5 Pyty/Shutterstock.com; p. 5 Rita Kochmarjova/Shutterstock.com; p. 7 (Satin Angora) Natalee Wright/Shutterstock.com; p. 7 (Giant Angora) Rayoclicks/Shutterstock.com; p. 7 (English Angora) Shal09/Shutterstock.com; p. 7 (French Angora) Evita Trankale/Shutterstock.com; p. 10 vetroff/Shutterstock.com; p. 11 Medvedev Andrey/Shutterstock.com; p. 13 pixelman/Shutterstock.com; p. 14, 15 Celiafoto/Shutterstock.com; p. 17 Elizabett/Shutterstock.com; p. 19 Irina Borsuchenko/Shutterstock.com; p. 21 sedan504/Shutterstock.com

Printed in the United States of America

CPSIA compliance information: Batch #CSGS23: For further information, contact Gareth Stevens, New York, New York, at 1-800-542-2595.

CONTENTS

Words in the glossary appear in **bold** type the first time they are used in the text.

FURRY RABBITS

Some of the softest, lightest, warmest **fabrics** in the world are simply called angora. We have Angora rabbits to thank for them! Angora rabbits come from Turkey. The name "Angora" is believed to have been taken from the original name of Ankara, which is the capital of Turkey.

Angora rabbits are easy to recognize by their long, soft fur. Depending on the rabbit, they may produce more than 1 pound (0.45 kg) of wool every year! Wool is the **fiber** that grows on an animal.

PULL BACK THE WOOL

The Angora goat also produces wool. It's called mohair.

Rabbits are nervous animals. It's important to be **gentle** when touching or holding a rabbit.

KINDS OF ANGORAS

The American Rabbit Breeders Association (ARBA) recognizes four kinds, or breeds, of Angora rabbits: English, French, satin, and giant Angoras.

The English Angora rabbit weighs about 7.5 pounds (3.4 kg). It's the smallest kind of Angora rabbit. Giant Angoras are the biggest of the breeds. Over time, people bred these big bunnies to be good at producing wool. Satin Angora rabbits grow shiny wool that has become some of the most prized wool out there.

PULL BACK THE WOOL

A fifth kind of Angora rabbit, the German Angora, is not recognized by the ARBA but shares features with the other kinds of Angora rabbits.

Each breed of Angora rabbit has its own special look—but they all grow beautiful wool!

COLORFUL CREATURES

No matter the breed, Angora rabbits may be lots of different colors. They can be black, white, chocolate, blue, lilac, and many shades in between. Rabbits that are called "blue" or "lilac" are shades of gray, rather than bright blue or purple. Angora rabbits may have blue, red, or brown eyes.

Angora rabbits born to the same parents can be different colors!

"Broken" rabbits have fur that's mostly white with spots of brown or black. "Pointed" rabbits have colors on their nose, ears, feet, and tail that differ from the main body color.

PULL BACK THE WOOL

Rabbit fur that has been **sheared** is sometimes called lapin.

RABBIT FAMILIES

All rabbits are mammals. Female rabbits are called does. Male rabbits are called bucks. Rabbits have babies very quickly. A mother Angora rabbit is **pregnant** for about a month before she has her babies, which are called kits or kittens. Angoras have litters of up to 15 kits at once!

Angora rabbit kits are very small and weak. Owners make sure a rabbit and her kits are in a safe place where predators, such as foxes, cats, or dogs, can't reach them.

PULL BACK THE WOOL

Angora rabbit kits are born without fur.

Mammals are animals that are **warm-blooded**, have hair or fur, and commonly give birth to live young that drink milk made by their mother.

ANGORA LIFE

A place where **domesticated** rabbits are kept is called a rabbitry. Rabbits like to **burrow**, so it's important not to keep them anywhere with a dirt floor. In most rabbitries, Angoras are kept in wire cages. Rabbits are happiest when they don't have to share their cage with others.

Angora rabbits eat rabbit food. Rabbit **pellets** are usually made of alfalfa, oats, and other vegetables and grains. Rabbits can also be fed carrots or fresh grass as small treats.

Rabbit owners don't put too much bedding inside a rabbit's cage. That could cause their fur to become matted and dirty.

KEPT FOR WOOL

For hundreds of years, Angora rabbits have been kept as pets and livestock. These animals are gentle, quiet, and fearful. They are easy to care for, but people who keep these rabbits must be very careful when handling them so as not to scare or harm them.

Today, farmers keep Angora rabbits to **harvest** their wool. There are small farms that have only a few rabbits. There are also large farms with many rabbits that produce a lot of wool!

China produces most of the world's Angora wool.

WOOL HARVEST

How Angora wool is harvested depends on the breed of Angora rabbit. German Angoras, which produce the most wool, are **sheared** about four times a year. English and French Angoras molt, or drop their coats, and the wool can be plucked right from their body by hand or using a brush.

Collecting the long hairs Angoras grow helps them. When Angoras swallow too much of their hair, they can get a sickness called wool block. Grooming helps keep wool block from happening.

PULL BACK THE WOOL

Angoras have layered fur. A layer of longer, coarser fur is called guard hair. The guard hair covers the rabbit's soft undercoat.

Angoras need to be groomed regularly even if owners don't plan to sell their wool.

WEAVING WOOL

Angora wool is seven times warmer than sheep's wool. It's perfect for making clothing such as scarves and sweaters, as well as blankets.

Spinning is the process by which Angora wool is made into yarn. Angora wool is very soft and thin. Spinning twists together two or more pieces of hair, making it stronger and tighter. Often, Angora fiber is combined with wool of other animals to make the yarn stronger. Weaving is the process by which yarn is made into fabric.

PULL BACK THE WOOL

Angora wool and alpaca wool are often combined to make soft yarn.

Goods made with Angora wool are popular in places that are cold.

RESPECTING THE RABBITS

Some people do not believe animal fur should be used to produce goods. They're worried about how the animals are kept and treated.

Angora rabbits are born into **captivity** and depend on people to care for them. Those that are kept in clean, happy homes become used to being sheared or plucked and will sit or lay quietly while their owner grooms them. Still, harvesting the wool of an Angora rabbit should be a gentle process that shows rabbits respect and care.

PULL BACK THE WOOL

Anyone interested in owning Angora rabbits or harvesting their wool should talk to other Angora farmers to learn to do it properly.

Angora wool and goods made from it can be sold for a lot of money.

GLOSSARY

burrow: To make a hole in which to live or hide.

captivity: The state of living in a place and not in the wild.

domesticated: Bred and raised for use by people.

fabric: A kind of cloth.

fiber: A thin thread of natural or human-made material that can be used to make cloth.

gentle: Not hard or forceful.

harvest: To gather or collect something for use.

pellet: A small, hard ball of food.

pregnant: Carrying an unborn baby in the body.

shear: To remove hair or wool from.

warm-blooded: Able to keep the body at a steady temperature no matter what the outside temperature is.

FOR MORE INFORMATION

Books

Dellaccio, Tanya. *Raising Llamas.* New York, NY: PowerKids Press, 2020.

Markovics, Joyce. *Angora Rabbit.* New York, NY: Bearport Publishing, 2016.

Websites

Angora Rabbit Breed Profiles

www.thesprucepets.com/angora-rabbit-breed-profiles-1835793

Find out more about each kind of Angora rabbit here.

Minnesota Zoo: Rabbit

mnzoo.org/blog/animals/rabbit/

Read more about rabbits, including Angora rabbits, here.

INDEX